# HEADLINES OF WORLD WAR II

## Nicola Barber

Evans Brothers Limited

This book is based on **1930s** and **1940s** by Ken Hills, first published by Evans Brothers Limited in 1992, but the original texts have been simplified.

Published by Evans Brothers Limited
2A Portman Mansions
Chiltern Street
London W1M 1LE

© Evans Brothers Limited 1994

First published 1994
Reprinted 1998

Typeset by Fleetlines Typesetters, Southend-on-Sea, Essex
Printed in Spain by GRAFO, S.A. – Bilbao

ISBN 0 237 51327 7

# Acknowledgements

Maps – Jillian Luff, Bitmap Graphics
Design – Neil Sayer
Editor – Su Swallow
Language adviser – Suzanne Tiburtius

For permission to reproduce copyright material the author and publishers gratefully acknowledge the following:

Cover photographs – (from top) The Illustrated London News Picture Company, The Vintage Magazine Company, Topham, Topham, The Hulton Picture Company.

Page 5 – (from top) Topham, Topham, Topham, Popperfoto; page 6 – (from top) Popperfoto, The Hulton Picture Company, The Vintage Magazine Co, The Vintage Magazine Co; page 7 – The Hulton Picture Company; page 8 – (left) The Hulton Picture Company, (right) Topham; page 9 – (left) Barnaby's Picture Library, (middle, top right) The Hulton Picture Company/The Bettmann Archive, (bottom right) The Illustrated London News Picture Library; page 10 – Topham; page 11 – (left) Penguin Books, (top) The Hulton Picture Company/The Bettmann Archive, (bottom) Topham; page 12 – Topham; page 13 – The Illustrated London News Picture Library; page 14 – (left, right) Topham, (top) The Vintage Magazine Co; page 16 – (top) Topham, (middle) The Hulton Picture Company/The Bettmann Archive, (bottom) Associated Press/Topham; page 17 – (left) Topham, (top right)

Barnaby's Picture Library, (bottom right) The Illustrated London News Picture Library; page 18 – Topham; page 19 – The Hulton Picture Company; page 20 – (top left) Colorsport, (bottom left) The Hulton Picture Company, (top right) The Vintage Magazine Co, (bottom right) Topham; page 21 – (left) The Hulton Picture Company, (right) Topham; page 22 – The Hulton Picture Company; page 24 – The Vintage Magazine Co; page 26 – (top) The Hulton Picture Company, (bottom) Ronald Sheridan/Ancient Art and Architecture Collection; page 27 – The Fine Art Society, London/Bridgeman Art Library; page 28 – The Vintage Magazine Co; page 29 – The Vintage Magazine Co; page 30 – (top) The Vintage Magazine Co, (bottom) Topham; page 31 – (top) The Hulton Picture Company, (bottom) Topham; page 32 – The Vintage Magazine Co; page 33 – Topham; page 34 – Topham; page 35 – (top) Topham, (bottom) The Hulton Picture Company; page 36 – (top) The Vintage Magazine Co, (bottom) Imperial War Museum, London/Bridgeman Art Library; page 37 – (left) Topham, (right) The Hulton Picture Company; page 38 – The Vintage Magazine Co; page 39 – (top) Topham, (bottom) the Hulton Picture Company; page 40 – The Hulton Picture Company; page 41 – (top) The Vintage Magazine Co, (bottom) Topham; page 42 – Topham; page 43 – The Vintage Magazine Co; page 44 – (left) The Vintage Magazine Co, (right) Topham; page 45 – (top) The Hulton Picture Company, (middle) Topham, (bottom) The Hulton Picture Company.

# Introduction

World War II began in September 1939 and ended in 1945. The war started in Europe when the German leader, Adolf Hitler, invaded Poland. Within a week Britain, Australia, New Zealand, South Africa, Canada and France had all declared war on Germany. Many other countries joined the fighting during the six years of the war. Over 55 million people died in the war. Many died in concentration camps. Bombs dropped in air raids also killed many other people.

The war ended when the USA dropped two atomic bombs on Japanese cities. After the war, the leaders of countries all around the world were determined to work for peace. They set up a new organisation called the United Nations to try to prevent more wars in the future.

The pictures on page 5 show:
Poster advertising 1936 Olympic Games in Berlin
Cover of British *Coronation Song Book*, 1937
Cover of *Mickey Mouse Annual*
Newspaper seller on the day Britain declared war, September 3, 1939

The pictures on page 6 show:
Winston Churchill, the British Prime Minister
The pilot of an RAF bomber plane
Nazi tanks stuck in the mud in Russia
Japanese officials surrendering on the American warship *Missouri* at the end of the war

# Contents

# 1933

Jan 30     **Hitler becomes Chancellor of Germany**
Feb 28     **Fire destroys German parliament**
March 20   **Concentration camps in Germany**

## New leader for Germany

**January 30, Berlin, Germany** The new leader of Germany is Adolf Hitler. Hitler is also leader of the Nazi party. The Nazis are enemies of the Communists and Jewish people. Many people are afraid that Hitler will now try to destroy these people.

△ Hitler (centre) with his ministers

## Fire burns down German parliament

**February 28, Berlin, Germany** Fire burnt down the German parliament building last night. The parliament building is called the Reichstag. Chancellor Hitler has blamed the Communists for the fire.

## Concentration camps

**March 20, Berlin, Germany** Places called concentration camps are planned in Germany. Anyone who speaks out against the Nazi government will be put in one of these camps. The first camp has already opened at Dachau.

## Countries walk out of League

**October 14, Geneva, Switzerland** Germany and Japan have walked out of the League of Nations. The League of Nations is an international organisation. It was set up after World War I to try to settle arguments in a peaceful way. But many people now think that the League does not have the power to keep the world at peace.

# 1934

## Austrian Chancellor is killed

**July 25, Vienna, Austria** The Austrian leader, Chancellor Dollfuss, was killed today. At noon, armed men went into the offices of Dr Dollfuss and shot him. They would not let a doctor in to see him and he bled to death. The armed men were members of the Austrian Nazi party.

The German leader, Adolf Hitler, has said that the German Nazi party had nothing to do with the killing. But many people think that Hitler had something to do with this crime.

▽ The body of the Austrian Chancellor, Dr Dollfuss, is guarded by two soldiers.

## Leading Nazis killed

**June 30, Munich, Germany** A leading Nazi, Ernst Roehm, has been killed. Some people think that other members of the Nazi party have also died elsewhere in Germany. It seems that Hitler himself ordered the murder of these people.

△ Adolf Hitler with some of his Nazi supporters

# News in brief . . .

## German children become Nazis

**Germany** When German boys are ten years old, they have to join the Young Peoples' Movement. They wear Nazi uniforms and learn to parade like soldiers. When they join the Movement they have to stand under a Nazi flag and say: "Under this flag, I swear to give all my strength to Adolf

△ German boys in the Young Peoples' Movement

Hitler, the man who saved our country. I am willing and ready to die for him, so help me God."

## A German greeting

**Germany** The Nazi government has ordered all Germans to greet each other in a new way. When two people meet they must hold up their right arms and say "Heil Hitler!" which means "Hail, Hitler!".

## Shorts at Wimbledon

**May, London, England** Women tennis players will be allowed to wear shorts instead of skirts at Wimbledon this year. Many male officials are

△ Women tennis players wearing shorts

upset by this new rule. They say that shorts are unsuitable for women to wear. They think that women who play at Wimbledon should set a good example.

## Dillinger dead

**July 22, Chicago, USA** The bank robber and murderer, John Dillinger, is dead. John Dillinger has killed 16 people. The police shot him as he came out of a cinema.

▽ John Dillinger, the bank robber and murderer

## *Queen Mary* launched

**September 26, Glasgow, Scotland** The ship called the *Queen Mary* was launched today. The *Queen Mary* is the first ship ever to weigh more than 75,000 tonnes.

▽ The launch of the *Queen Mary*

# 1935

March 16     **Hitler tears up Versailles treaty**
May     **Threat of war in East Africa**
October 3     **Italy invades Abyssinia**

## Hitler tears up treaty

**March 16, Berlin, Germany** Hitler has torn up the Versailles Treaty. This was the agreement that ended World War I. The Treaty said that Germany could have a small army and navy, and no airforce. Now Hitler has ignored the treaty and started to build up Germany's armed forces.

## War in East Africa

**May, East Africa** It seems likely that there will be a war in East Africa. The Italian leader, Mussolini, has sent troops to Italian East Africa. They are now on the border between East Africa and Abyssinia.

△ The Abyssinian army gets ready for war.

## Italy invades Abyssinia

**October 3, East Africa** Italian troops crossed the border into Abyssinia this morning. The Italians have modern weapons. Many of the Abyssinians only have spears and bows and arrows to fight with.

△ Italian troops leave for East Africa.

# News in brief...

## Dust storms in America

**April 15, USA** Strong winds have blown clouds of dust across farmland in America (see right). The dust has ruined many crops. Thousands of people have left their homes because they cannot grow any food.

## A new world record

**September 3, Bonneville Salt Flats, Utah, USA** Sir Malcolm Campbell has set a new world record for the fastest speed on land. He went at 301 miles (484 kms) per hour in his car *Bluebird*. This is the eighth time Campbell has broken the world record.

## Good books for everyone

**July, London** Penguin books are in the shops. 'Penguin' is the name of a new family of books published by Mr Allen Lane. The books are paperbacks. They cost only sixpence (two new pence) each.

## First performance of *Porgy and Bess*

**September 30, Boston, USA** The opera *Porgy and Bess* has its first performance today. *Porgy and Bess* is by George Gershwin. There are many fine tunes in the opera, including the song *Summertime*.

## Nazis ban jazz music

**October, Berlin** The Nazis have banned all jazz music played by black people or Jewish people in Germany. The Nazis say that this jazz music has a bad effect on young Germans.

# 1936

## New king for Britain

**January 20, London, England** King George V has died. He had been on the throne for 25 years. The king's eldest son, Edward, becomes King Edward VIII.

▽ A poster showing the power of American industry

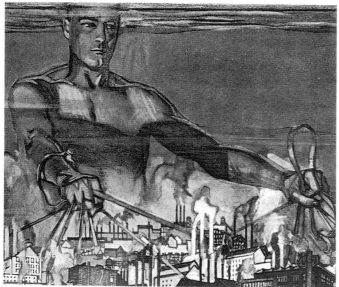

## Roosevelt wins again

**November 3, Washington, USA** The American people have elected Franklin D. Roosevelt to be their president for the second time. Roosevelt has been president since 1933. He is very popular with the American people.

## A king in love

**December 10, London, England** The new king is in love with Mrs Wallis Simpson. She is an American who has been married twice before. The king is not allowed to marry someone who has been married before. So King Edward VIII has decided to abdicate. This means that he has given up the throne. His brother will become the new king instead.

Many people have tried to persuade King Edward to leave Mrs Simpson. But he will not change his mind. He has chosen to give up the throne in order to marry Mrs Simpson.

## The new royal family

**December 12, London, England** King Edward VIII has left the country. His new title is the Duke of Windsor. His brother is now the new King George VI. King George and his wife Queen Elizabeth have two daughters, Princess Elizabeth and Princess Margaret. Princess Elizabeth is ten years old.

# Civil war in Spain

**SPANISH CIVIL WAR (July/August 1936)**

N

Santander
Guernica
FRANCE
Bilbao
Vigo
Burgos
(Nationalist
Government
Headquarters)
CATALONIA
Barcelona
Salamanca
Madrid
PORTUGAL
SPAIN
Minorca
Majorca
Lisbon
Ibiza

Seville
Granada
ATLANTIC
OCEAN
Cadiz
Gibraltar
Tangier
(British)
0  km  250
SPANISH MOROCCO

Initial advance of Nationalists
Nationalist territory
Republican territory

**July 31, Spain** A civil war has started in Spain. A civil war is when people from the same country fight against each other. The Spanish army has attacked the Spanish government and its supporters. The leader of the Spanish army is General Franco. He says that the government is turning Spain into a Communist country. He has started a new political party to fight against Communism. It is called the Nationalist party.

People who are on the side of the Spanish government are called Republicans. The Republicans have formed an army of their own. But the Republican army does not have as many weapons as Franco's army. Fighting between the Republicans and the Nationalists is going on all over Spain.

# Italy occupies Abyssinia

**May 9, Abyssinia** Italian soldiers have reached Addis Ababa, the capital of Abyssinia. The Italians are in control of Addis Ababa. This means that the country of Abyssinia now belongs to Italy. The emperor of Abyssinia has escaped and gone abroad. The king of Italy will now be called 'Emperor of Abyssinia'.

# German troops enter Rhineland

**March 6, Rhineland** German soldiers have gone into the Rhineland. The Rhineland is an area of land between France and Germany. After World War I this area was used to keep the two countries apart. There were to be no troops in this area. People are very unhappy that the German troops have ignored this agreement. Now many people think that Germany wants to start another war.

△ Republican fighters in Barcelona

# News in brief...

## A new car for Germany

**February 26, Wolfsburg, Germany** Hitler has opened a new factory in Wolfsburg. The factory will make a cheap family car. This car will be called 'The People's Car'. Its German name is *Volkswagen*.

▷ The new German car, the *Volkswagen*

## Jesse Owens wins medals

**August 15, Berlin, Germany** The eleventh Olympic Games ended today. The black American runner, Jesse Owens, won four gold medals. The Nazis are very angry about this. The Nazis say that white people are better than black people. But a black runner has shown everyone that he is the best in the world.

▽ Jesse Owens

## King Edward's speech

**December 11, London, England** Edward VIII made his last speech as king this evening. The speech was broadcast on the radio. This is part of what he said: "I want you to understand that in making up my mind I did not forget the country or the Empire which as Prince of Wales and lately as king, I have for 25 years tried to serve. But you must believe me when I tell you that I have found it impossible to carry the heavy bur-

△ King Edward makes his last speech.

den of responsibility and to discharge my duties as king as I would wish to do without the help and support of the woman I love..."

# 1937

## Fighting in Spain

**February, Spain** People from other countries are fighting in the Civil War in Spain. Italian and German troops are helping General Franco and the Nationalists. The Russians are helping the Republicans.

## Guernica bombed

**April 26, northern Spain** This is how a reporter described what he found in the city of Guernica after the German bombing:

'In the Plaza, surrounded almost by a wall of fire, were about a hundred refugees. They were wailing and weeping and rocking to and fro. One middle-aged man spoke English. He told me, "At four, before the market closed, many aeroplanes came. They dropped bombs. Some came low and shot bullets into the streets. . .".'

(Noel Monks, *Eyewitness*, Frederick Muller 1955)

## Spanish city destroyed

**April 30, northern Spain** Bombs have destroyed the city of Guernica (see map page 13). Guernica is in part of northern Spain held by the Republicans. The bombs were dropped by German planes. The Germans are fighting on the side of General Franco and the Nationalists.

It was market day in Guernica when the Germans dropped the bombs. Fires and explosions killed over 2000 people in Guernica. The people had no warning that the Germans were going to attack. People all round the world are shocked and angry about the bombing.

## George VI crowned

**May 12, London, England** King George and Queen Elizabeth were crowned this morning in Westminster Abbey. The king and queen's two daughters watched the crowning. Afterwards the royal family went back to Buckingham Palace and waved from the balcony to the huge crowds below.

# News in brief . . .

## Giant airship explodes

**May 6, Lakehurst Airfield, USA** The giant airship *Hindenburg* has exploded. The German airship had just crossed the Atlantic Ocean. It was about to stop at its mooring mast. Suddenly the airship caught fire and the gas inside the airship exploded. All 34 people on board died in the flames.

Only last year the *Hindenburg* had set a new record for the fastest crossing of the Atlantic. It had crossed the ocean in under two days. The Germans were hoping to start a regular passenger service across the Atlantic Ocean.

## The terror of war

**October, Paris, France** The Spanish artist, Pablo Picasso, has painted a picture in protest at the bombing of Guernica earlier this year. His picture reminds people of the terror of war.

## New boxing champion

**June 3, New York, USA** The American boxer, Joe Louis (see right), is the new heavyweight boxing champion of the world. Joe Louis is the first black boxer to be champion for 22 years.

▷ Picasso's painting, *Guernica*

# 1938

# Hitler threatens war

**September 27, Germany** Adolf Hitler wants parts of Czechoslovakia to become part of Germany. The British Prime Minister, Neville Chamberlain, has gone to Munich to try to persuade Hitler not to go to war.

△ Prime Minister Neville Chamberlain (right) with Adolf Hitler

△ A picture of Adolf Hitler on a German poster

# Churchill says, "Don't give in"

**September 28, London, England** A member of the British parliament, Winston Churchill, has said that Chamberlain should not give in to Hitler. He says that Britain and France should fight if Germany attacks Czechoslovakia. Many people agree with Winston Churchill.

△ Preparing for war in London. Sandbags protect a police station against bombs.

# Chamberlain returns from Munich

△ Neville Chamberlain returns from Munich.

**September 30, London, England** Crowds of people welcomed Prime Minister Chamberlain as he came back from Munich this evening. Chamberlain waved a piece of paper signed by Hitler and himself. He said that Britain and Germany would not go to war. "It is peace for our time," he said.

The leaders of France, Italy and Britain have agreed that Germany can take over parts of Czechoslovakia. In return, Hitler has said that he will leave the Czech people in peace. Many people are relieved because a war now looks unlikely. But the Czech people are unhappy about this agreement.

# German troops invade Austria

**March 14, Vienna, Austria** German troops have crossed into Austria. People cheered as Hitler drove through the streets of Vienna, the Austrian capital.

The Austrian leader, Seyss Inquart, is a member of the Nazi party. He invited the Germans to invade Austria. Many Austrians would like their country to become part of Germany.

Germany is now the most powerful country in Europe.

# Germans attack Austrian Jews

**March 18, Vienna, Austria** The Germans have attacked the Jews living in Austria. The Germans have said that no Jewish person is allowed to be a lawyer, doctor or teacher.

△ The Nazis have smashed the windows of shops owned by Jews.

# Danger of war over Czechoslovakia

**May 20, Prague, Czechoslovakia** Once again, there is a threat of war. German troops now surround Czechoslovakia on three sides (see map). There are many Germans living in Czechoslovakia. They say that the Czech people treat them badly. They have asked Germany for protection.

If Germany does invade Czechoslovakia it will break the agreement made between Chamberlain and Hitler. It is hard to see how Britain and France could avoid going to war against Germany if this happens.

# Franco winning Spanish war

**April 15, Spain** General Franco claims that he is winning the Spanish Civil War. It seems that the Republicans must face defeat.

# 'Kristallnacht'

**November 11, Berlin, Germany** Two nights ago mobs attacked Jews all over Germany. Thousands of Jewish shops were smashed and robbed. There was so much broken glass on the streets that the Germans have called it "Kristallnacht" – 'the night of broken glass'.

**GERMANY ATTACKS CZECHOSLOVAKIA**

N

DENMARK
USSR
BRITAIN
London
NETH.
Danzig
Berlin
GERMANY
POLAND
BELGIUM
Rhine
Prague
CZECHOSLOVAKIA
Paris
Vienna
SWITZERLAND
AUSTRIA
HUNGARY
FRANCE
Danube
0  km  500
German-speaking areas of Czechoslovakia
YUGOSLAVIA
ITALY

# News in brief . . .

## Snow White success

**January, Hollywood, USA**
Walt Disney's new film *Snow White and the Seven Dwarfs* is a great success. *Snow White* is the first full-length cartoon film to be made.

## Italy wins World Cup

**June 19, Paris, France** The Italian football team has won the World Cup in the final in Paris.

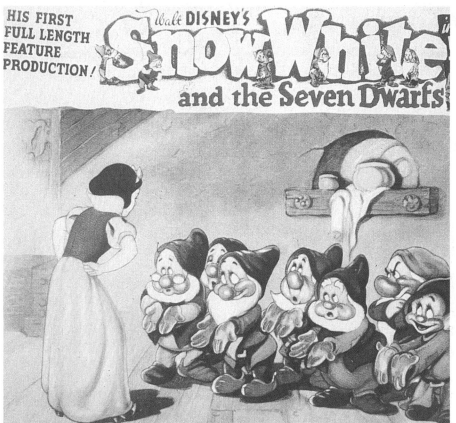

## Britain orders more planes

**July 15, London, England** The British government has ordered 1000 new planes for the Royal Air Force. The planes are called Spitfires.

▽ A Spitfire plane

## British get gas masks

**September 20, London, England** Everyone in Britain is to get a free gas mask. The masks are to protect against poison gas from bombs.

▽ Children carry their new gas masks.

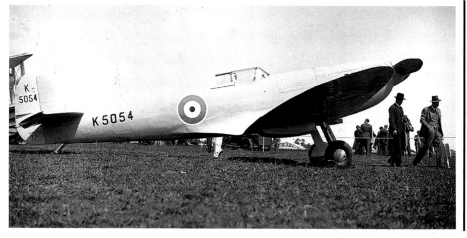

# 1939

## Hitler invades Czechoslovakia

**March 15, Berlin, Germany** Hitler has invaded Czechoslovakia. Two days ago he sent a list of demands to the Czech government. The Czechs did not give in to Hitler's demands. So Hitler has used this as an excuse to move troops into Czechoslovakia.

△ Germans cheer as Hitler returns to Berlin after the invasion of Czechoslovakia.

## Czech people weep as Germans enter Prague

**March 16, Prague, Czechoslovakia** Czechs showed their anger as the Germans entered their capital city, Prague, today. Some people stood silently, some hissed and booed, some shook their fists. Some wept to see the hated enemy in their country. The German soldiers forced the people to give the Nazi salute. All cafés, restaurants, theatres and cinemas are to be closed.

△ People in Prague are forced to salute like Nazis.

21

# Czech invasion shocks the world

**March 17** Hitler's invasion of Czechoslovakia has shocked the whole world. Only six months ago, Hitler promised in Munich to leave Czechoslovakia alone. Now he has made the country part of Germany. Both the British and French governments have sent letters to Berlin protesting about the hostile German invasion.

# Russia and Germany sign agreement

**August 23, Moscow, USSR** Russia and Germany have signed an agreement not to go to war against each other. This is bad news for Britain and France. If necessary, they were hoping to persuade Russia to join them against Germany.

POLAND ATTACKED

German and Russian attacks

Polish Corridor - a narrow strip of land which is Poland's route or 'corridor' to the sea

# Hitler threatens Poland

**March 31, Berlin, Germany** Hitler is now threatening Poland. He wants the Poles to give up the city of Danzig to Germany. Danzig used to be a German city. But it became part of Poland after World War I. Now Hitler wants the city back.

Britain and France have promised to help Poland if Germany attacks.

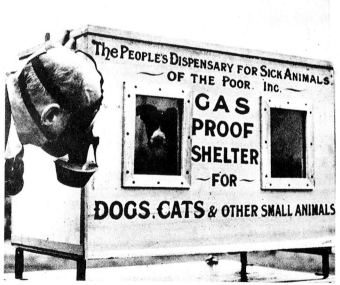

The People's Dispensary for Sick Animals of the Poor. Inc.
GAS PROOF SHELTER
— FOR —
DOGS. CATS & OTHER SMALL ANIMALS

△ A shelter for animals to protect them from gas in an air raid

# Europe gets ready for war

**August 31, London, England** Europe is getting ready for war. In Poland, France and Britain thousands of young men have left their jobs to join the armed forces.

# Germany invades Poland

**September 1, Poland** German troops invaded Poland early this morning. They pulled down barriers along the border and crossed into Poland.

# Russia attacks Poland

**September 17, Poland** Russian troops have invaded Poland. They are trying to occupy as much of the country as they can before the Germans get there. The Polish army is trapped between the two invaders.

# Britain and France go to war

**September 3, London, England** Britain and France are at war with Germany. Prime Minister Chamberlain gave the news to the British people in a radio broadcast at 11.15 this morning.

# British troops land in France

**September 27, France** About 150,000 troops have landed in France. They will help the French to fight against the Germans.

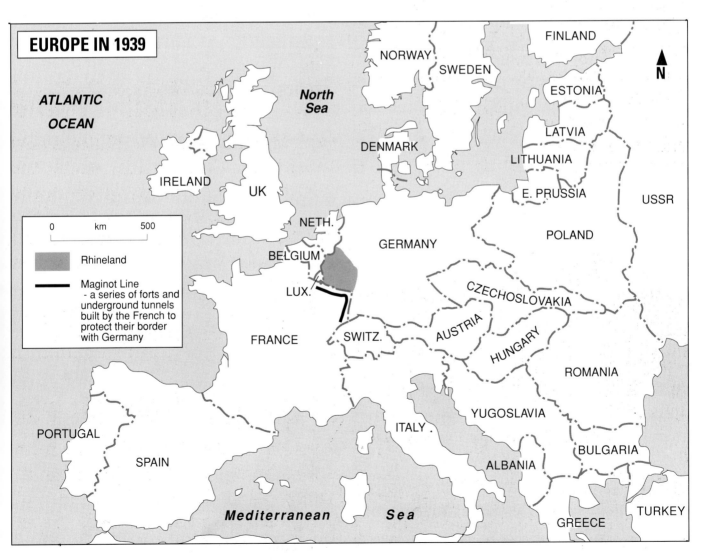

EUROPE IN 1939

ATLANTIC OCEAN

0 km 500

Rhineland

Maginot Line
- a series of forts and underground tunnels built by the French to protect their border with Germany

# Spanish Civil War ends

**March 28, Madrid, Spain** General Franco has won the Civil War in Spain. He has beaten the Republicans and the war is over. But there are many problems for Franco. The war destroyed many towns and cities as well as factories. Many farm animals died. The whole country needs rebuilding, but Spain is now a poor country.

# British children moved to safety

**September 2, London, England** Many British children from the towns and cities are moving to the safety of the countryside. The children are leaving their homes to stay with families in the countryside. This is because the Germans are likely to bomb the cities. The countryside is safer.

# German battleship sinks

**December 17, Montevideo, Uruguay** The German battleship, the *Graf Spee*, has sunk. Her own crew blew the ship up. This is because British warships were waiting for the *Graf Spee* as she left the harbour in Montevideo. There was no escape for the German ship. The Royal Navy has been looking for the *Graf Spee* for weeks.

# Children moved from London

**September 1, London, England** Moving people away from a dangerous place to a safer place is called evacuation. This is a description of the evacuation of some children from a school in London: 'I watched the schoolteachers calling out their names and tying luggage labels on their coats, checking their parcels to see there were warm and clean clothes . . . mothers and fathers were saying goodbye, straightening the girls' hair, getting the boys to blow their noses and lightly and quickly kissing them . . . There was quite a long wait before this small army got its orders . . . to move off . . .

Labelled and lined up the children began to move out of the school.'

(Hilde Marchant, *Women and Children Last*, published by Victor Gollancz Ltd, 1941)

# 1940

| | |
|---|---|
| May 10 | Churchill new British leader |
| May 13 | Germans advance into France |
| June 4 | Rescue from Dunkirk |
| June 19 | Germans enter Paris |
| August 20 | Battle of Britain |

## German invasions

**May 10, Oslo, Norway** German troops invaded Norway and Denmark in April. The Germans took the Danes by surprise. The Danes were not ready to fight so they surrendered to the Germans. There was fighting in Oslo, the Norwegian capital. But a Norwegian Nazi called Quisling took control of the country for the Germans. Now most of Norway is controlled by the Germans. British and French troops have landed in Norway to try to drive the Germans out. But so far they have not succeeded.

## New leader for Britain

**May 10, London, England** Winston Churchill has replaced Neville Chamberlain as leader of Britain. Many people blame Neville Chamberlain for Britain's failure to save Norway from the Germans. Winston Churchill will form a National Government made up of people from all political parties.

## German advances continue

**May 13, France** German troops are still advancing across Europe. They have invaded Holland, Luxembourg and Belgium. Germany is now attacking France. Britain and France are now making plans to fight back.

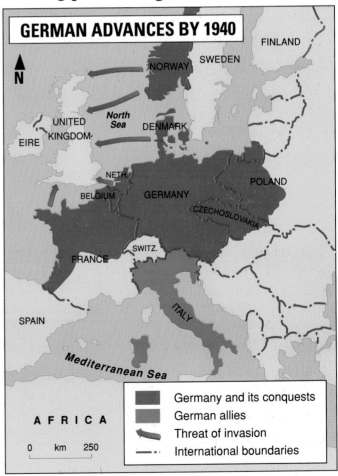

By 1940 the Germans had taken much of Europe.

# British army trapped in Dunkirk

**May 29, France** German forces have reached the French coast along the Channel. The British army is trapped in the port of Dunkirk. The only way out is by sea.

# Cave discovery

**November 1, Lascaux, France** Some French boys have made an amazing discovery. They were catching rabbits when they saw a gap in some rocks. They went through the gap and found a cave. Paintings covered the cave walls. Experts say that the paintings are 15,000 years old.

# Rescue from Dunkirk

**June 4, London, England** Hundreds of little ships have gone to the rescue of the British army. The ships sailed across the Channel to Dunkirk. They brought back over 300,000 British troops to Britain.

△ British troops waiting at Dunkirk

▽ Cave paintings in Lascaux

# Paris falls to Germans

**June 19, London, England** The Germans have occupied Paris. The Germans now control much of France. But some French people are determined to go on fighting against the Germans. This movement against the Germans is called the Resistance. The Resistance is led by General Charles de Gaulle from London.

# RAF is unbeaten

**August 20, London, England** The Royal Air Force (RAF) is fighting a fierce war against the German airforce (the Luftwaffe). German troops are waiting to invade Britain. But they must wait until the Luftwaffe has destroyed the British defences.

# RAF saves Britain

**September 19, London, England** The RAF says it shot down 185 Luftwaffe planes in air battles on September 15. The RAF seems to have beaten the Luftwaffe in the 'Battle of Britain'. Hitler has given up his plans to invade Britain. The RAF has saved Britain.

△ A painting called *The Battle of Britain* by Paul Nash

# News in brief . . .

## Roosevelt wins again

**November 5, Washington, USA** Once again, Americans have voted for Franklin D. Roosevelt to be their president. This is the third time that Roosevelt has been elected. This is good news for Britain because Roosevelt is a strong supporter of its war efforts.

## Children go home

**January 30, London, England** When the war started last September many children from the cities went to live in the countryside. People thought it would be safer there. But many children did not like living in the countryside. They missed their parents. So many have now gone home, back to the cities.

## Tragedy in the Atlantic

**September 22, London, England** There has been a tragedy in the Atlantic Ocean. The ship *City of Benares* was sailing to America to take many children away from the dangers of war in Britain. But a German submarine sunk the *City of Benares*. Ships have picked up 46 children, but 306 have drowned.

# Pets at war

"Send your pets to the country if you can. If you cannot, remember that your dog will not be allowed to go into a public air raid shelter with you. So don't take him shopping with you. Take him for walks near home, so that you can get back quickly.

Cats can take care of themselves far better than you can. Your cat will probably meet you when you get into the shelter."

(BBC broadcast on how to look after your pets during wartime.)

## Nights underground

**September 30, London, England** Thousands of people in London spend their nights in Underground stations. They

△ People sleeping in the Underground

are sheltering from the German air raids. But the Underground stations are very dirty, as this girl describes:

"Dirt abounds everywhere. The floors are never swept and are filthy. People are sleeping on piles of rubbish."

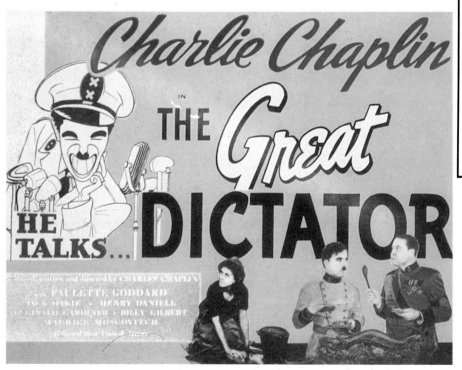

## The Great Dictator

**November 11, London, England** *The Great Dictator* is a new film by Charlie Chaplin. The film makes fun of the German leader, Adolf Hitler.

# 1941

## Germans invade Russia

**October 26, Moscow, USSR** In June, Hitler attacked the USSR. Three million troops with 3000 tanks crossed the Russian border. The Russian leader, Stalin, ordered people to burn or destroy anything that would be useful to the Germans including crops, animals and machines. The Germans are now moving towards the capital of the USSR, Moscow. But rain has made all the roads very muddy. The Germans are struggling to keep moving forwards.

## Germans freeze in Russian winter

**December 2, Moscow, USSR** The German army is freezing in the cold Russian winter. Russian troops are now attacking the Germans and forcing them to go back.

## The war at sea

**May 27, North Atlantic Ocean** The Royal Navy sank the huge German battle ship the *Bismarck* today. The *Bismarck* had attacked many of the sh that carried food and other sup from America to Britain.

△ A painting called *The End of the Bismarck* by Charles E. T

# Attack at Pearl Harbor

**December 7, Honolulu, Hawaii** In a surprise attack, Japanese planes have bombed American ships at Pearl Harbor in Hawaii. The bombs killed over 2000 people. The USA and Britain have declared war on Japan.

△ Japanese planes attack American ships at Pearl Harbor.

# War in the desert

**April 11, Libya** Earlier this year troops from Britain and other friendly countries (called the Allies) advanced against the Italian army in North Africa. Now German soldiers have taken over from the Italian army. The Germans are attacking the Allied troops fiercely.

# rmans retreat in Africa

**ber 10, Libya** The Allies are ng back against the German They have pushed the Germans where they were in April.

# The Japanese advance

**December 25, Hong Kong** Japanese forces have landed in Thailand, Malaya and the Philippines. They now control the American island of Guam in the Pacific Ocean. Today the Japanese have also taken Hong Kong.

# Women at work

**December 30, Britain** Women are doing the jobs left by male workers who have gone to fight in the war. The government first asked women to help in March. Now, some women are working in factories, others are working on farms. Many women have also joined the armed forces. They have to work very hard, but are glad to help. Many women have never done this kind of work before.

△ Women workers on the farms are called land girls.

# News in brief . . .

## Amy Johnson missing

**January 8, London, England** Amy Johnson is missing. People think she may have drowned in the Thames when her plane crashed. Amy Johnson became famous when she flew on her own from Britain to Australia before the war.

## First boy scout dies

**January 8, London, England** Lord Baden Powell has died. He was 83 years old. Lord Baden Powell started the Boy Scouts in 1908 and the Girl Guides in 1910.

## Comfort in the Underground

**February 28, London, England** Conditions have improved for people in the Underground. Every night people shelter in Underground stations from the bombs. Now the government has put in bunk beds for people to sleep on. Some stations have cookers and kettles for people to make food and drinks.

# Britain and America sign agreement

**August 14, London, England** President Roosevelt and Prime Minister Churchill have held a secret meeting at sea. They signed an agreement to continue fighting until they beat their enemies. The agreement is called the Atlantic Charter.

△ Roosevelt and Churchill meet on board HMS *Prince of Wales*.

# The Blitz in London

**May 31, London, England** The German bombing of London is called the Blitz. In the Blitz, bombs have damaged nearly four million houses in Britain and destroyed about 200,000 more. Many thousands of people have no home.

▽ Many houses have been damaged in the Blitz.

# 1942

May 10      Japan takes control of Philippines
May 31      RAF bombs Cologne
August 31   Germans enter Stalingrad
November 2  British win in Africa
November 23 Germans trapped in Stalingrad

## RAF bombs Cologne

**May 31, Cologne, Germany** More than a thousand RAF planes have dropped bombs on the city of Cologne. The bombs destroyed most of the city.

## Germans in Stalingrad

**November 23, Stalingrad, USSR** German troops have been in Stalingrad since August and are dying of hunger and cold. Most of the city is in ruins.

△ Ruined houses in Stalingrad

△ Ruins in the centre of the city

△ The Russians left their guns behind.

△ German troops advance

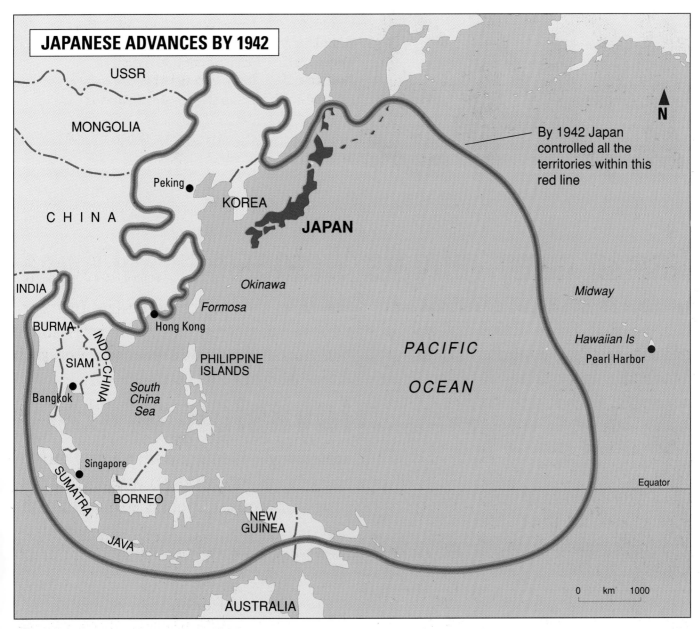

**JAPANESE ADVANCES BY 1942**

USSR

MONGOLIA

Peking

CHINA

KOREA

JAPAN

By 1942 Japan controlled all the territories within this red line

N

INDIA

Okinawa

Formosa

Midway

BURMA

Hong Kong

Hawaiian Is
Pearl Harbor

SIAM

INDO-CHINA

PHILIPPINE
ISLANDS

PACIFIC

OCEAN

Bangkok

South
China
Sea

Singapore

SUMATRA

BORNEO

Equator

JAVA

NEW
GUINEA

0    km    1000

AUSTRALIA

# Japan marches on

**May 10, Philippine Islands** The Japanese army has had many successes in the Pacific and southeast Asia. The Japanese control Singapore and the Philippines. Now they are threatening India.

# British win in Africa

**November 2, Cairo, Egypt** The British have won a ten-day battle against the Germans at El Alamein in Africa. Under their new commander, General Montgomery, British troops are now chasing the German troops as they retreat westwards.

▽ General Montgomery (centre)

# 1943

May 13        Germans surrender in North Africa
September 3   Allies invade Italy
December 31   German army retreats in USSR
December 31   Gustav Line stops Allies in Italy

## German army retreats

**December 31, USSR**  The German army is retreating from Russia. The Germans have not been able to defeat the Russian army. The Russian army stopped the Germans from capturing Kursk in July. Then the Russians took the city of Kiev from the Germans. Now the Germans are retreating. The Russians are driving the enemy out of their country. So far they have pushed the Germans back 300 kilometres.

## Victory in North Africa

**May 13, Tunisia**  The Allied troops have won a victory in North Africa. The German forces were trapped by the Allies and have given up.

## Invasion of Italy

**September 3, Messina, Italy**  The British army and its Allies have landed in southern Italy. They are fighting the German army in Italy. The government of Italy wants to make peace with the Allies.

△ The British army cross the Sangro River in Italy.

# The war against Japan

**December 29, Solomon Islands, Pacific Ocean** The Americans are slowly capturing the islands around Japan. But the Japanese soldiers fight until they are killed. They do not give up. Many Americans have also died.

# Allies fight on in Italy

**December 31, Italy** The American and British armies are still fighting the Germans in Italy. The Germans are fighting very fiercely. The Allies have reached a line of German defences across Italy. This is called the Gustav Line. Progress has been very slow, and the Gustav Line has stopped the Allies advancing any further.

# Allied leaders meet in Persia

**November 28, Tehran, Persia** The three leaders of the Allied forces are meeting in Persia. They are planning what to do next in the war.

△ Stalin, Roosevelt and Churchill in Persia

## Germans attack ghetto

**June 30, Warsaw, Poland** On April 19, German troops attacked the Jewish ghetto in Warsaw. The ghetto is the part of the city where the Germans made all the Jewish people live. Now the Germans are taking the Jews to concentration camps. About 7000 Jews have died fighting the Germans.

▷ German troops force Polish Jews out of the ghetto in Warsaw.

# 1944

## US General to lead Allies

**January 16, London, England** The American General, Dwight D. Eisenhower, is to lead the Allies. Eisenhower is known as 'Ike'. The Allies are getting ready to invade Europe and attack the Germans.

▷ Eisenhower with some of his troops

## 'D-Day' in France

**June 6, Normandy, France** Today is 'D-Day' and the Allies have landed in France. The Germans are fighting fiercely. But the Allies have been fighting back.

## Allies advance in France

**August 20, Falaise, France** On August 2, American troops advanced into France. Now, 50,000 Germans are trapped by the Americans around the town of Falaise.

△ A painting by Barnett Freedman showing the Allies landing in France.

# Plans for peace

**September 16, Quebec, Canada** The Allies are planning a better world when the war is over. President Roosevelt and Prime Minister Churchill have agreed to start a new organisation for keeping the world at peace. It will be called the United Nations Organisation.

# Paris is free

**August 26, Paris, France** Paris is free. The Allied troops have forced the Germans to leave. French soldiers were the first to enter the city. People cheered and waved as General Charles de Gaulle led the troops.

△ General Charles de Gaulle in Paris

# The war in Italy

**December 9, Rimini, Italy** The Allied forces have pushed the Germans into northern Italy. But many Allied troops are now leaving Italy and going to fight on the borders of Germany.

# Thousands killed in Warsaw

**October 9, Warsaw, Poland** It is thought that the Germans have killed 200,000 Polish people in Warsaw. The Poles tried to attack the Germans. But the Germans killed the Poles and destroyed all the buildings in Warsaw.

△ The ruins of Warsaw

# Russian victories

**December 1, Belgrade, Yugoslavia** The Russian army has had many victories this year. The Russians have beaten the Germans in Romania, Bulgaria, Hungary and Yugoslavia. As the Germans have left, the Russians have put in their own rulers in these countries. These rulers are controlled by the Soviet government in Moscow. The Russians are quickly building up a new Soviet empire.

# 1945

May 1       **Hitler kills himself**
May 8       **Germany surrenders; VE Day**
August 7       **Atomic bomb dropped on Hiroshima**
August 15       **Japan surrenders**

## Allies cross the Rhine

**March 31, River Rhine, Germany** American, British and Canadian troops have crossed the River Rhine in Germany. They are about to meet up with troops from the Russian army. The Allied and Russian armies will attack the Germans. The war in Europe is about to end.

## Battles in Berlin

**April 24, Berlin, Germany** The Russian army has reached the German capital, Berlin. The Russians have surrounded the city. Hitler is hiding in an underground shelter somewhere in the city. Hitler still thinks that Germany can win the war. He is still giving orders to his armies. But he has only a million men to defend Berlin. Many are young boys, others are old men. The German airforce, the Luftwaffe, no longer exists.

△ The Russian flag flies in Berlin over the Reichstag, the parliament building.

## Hitler is dead

**May 1, Berlin, Germany** Hitler is dead. He killed himself yesterday in his underground shelter in Berlin. The Italian leader, Mussolini, is also dead. He was shot three days ago.

## Germany surrenders

**May 8, Rheims, France** The German leaders have surrendered to General Eisenhower in Rheims. The war in Europe is over. But the war with Japan continues.

△ A survivor from the Belsen concentration camp

# London celebrates victory

**May 8, London, England**  Today is Victory in Europe Day. It is called VE Day for short. The centre of London is full of people singing, dancing and cheering. The royal family stood on the balcony at Buckingham Palace this afternoon. They waved to the crowds of cheering people below. In Whitehall Prime Minister Churchill came out to see the crowd. The people sang 'For He's a Jolly Good Fellow' to him.

△ Celebrations in London on VE day

# Inside the Belsen concentration camp

**April 15, Belsen, Germany**  When the first Allied soldiers went into the concentration camps in Germany they were horrified by what they saw. Many thousands of Jewish people died in the concentration camps. This is how one soldier described what he saw:

"About 35,000 corpses were reckoned, more actually than the living. Of the living, there were about 30,000 . . .

The camp was so full because people had been brought here from east and west. Some people were brought from Nordhausen, a five-day journey, without food. Many had marched for two or three days. There was no food at all in the camp, a few piles of roots (vegetables) – amidst the piles of dead bodies. Some of the dead bodies were of people so hungry that though the roots were guarded by SS-men they had tried to storm them and had been shot down. There was no water. . ."

(Derek Sington, political officer, reported by Patrick Gordon-Walker in *Book of Reportage*, Faber 1987)

# The forgotten war

**May 19, Thailand** British and Indian troops have driven the Japanese out of India and Burma. They are now about to invade Thailand. The British and Indian forces are led by General 'Bill' Slim. But in Europe many people have forgotten about the war in these countries. The papers have only written about the struggles in Europe and the Pacific.

# Hiroshima destroyed

**August 7, Washington, USA** The Americans have dropped a new kind of bomb on the city of Hiroshima in Japan. An American B29 Superfortress plane dropped the bomb yesterday. It exploded with a huge, purple ball of fire. A dark cloud, shaped like a mushroom, rose from the bomb. This was an atomic bomb. It destroyed the city of Hiroshima. The bomb killed and injured thousands of people. The American President, Harry S. Truman, has threatened Japan with more atomic bombs unless it surrenders.

# Japan surrenders

**August 15, Tokyo, Japan** On August 9, the Americans dropped another atomic bomb. It fell on Nagasaki in Japan and killed thousands of people. The Emperor of Japan has surrendered. This means that World War II is finally over.

△ Hiroshima after the bomb

# Death in Hiroshima

**September 9, Hiroshima, Japan** This is a description of what happened when the atomic bomb dropped on Hiroshima: "Within a few seconds the thousands of people in the streets and the gardens in the centre of the town were scorched by a wave of searing heat. Many were killed instantly, others lay writhing on the ground screaming in agony from the intolerable pain of their burns. Trams were picked up and tossed aside as though they had neither weight nor solidity. Trains were flung off the rails as though they were toys. Horses, dogs and cattle suffered the same fate as human beings. Even the vegetation did not escape."

(Marcel Junod, *Warrior without Weapons*, Jonathan Cape 1951)

# News in brief . . .

## President dies suddenly

**April 12, Washington, USA**
President Roosevelt died suddenly today. The Vice-President Harry S. Truman will become the new president of the United States.

## Lights shine in Britain

**July 15, London, England**
The blackout in Britain is over. During the blackout no lights were allowed at night in the streets, in shops or in buildings. The blackout made it more difficult for German planes to see where towns and cities were. Now streets and shops are lit up again.

## Countries work for peace

**October 24, New York, USA**
Twenty-nine countries have signed the United Nations Charter. This is an agreement to try to prevent war in the future.

▷ The symbol of the new United Nations.

## Labour party win election

**July 26, London, England**
The Labour party has won the British election. The leader of the Labour party is Clement Attlee.

▷ Clement Attlee, the leader of the Labour party

# Germany and Berlin split up

**August 2, Potsdam, Germany**   The Allies are splitting Germany up. Different countries will control different areas of Germany. Leaders of the Allied countries are meeting at Potsdam. They have decided that Russia will take over the eastern half of Germany. The Americans, the British and the French will run the rest of the country. The German capital, Berlin, will be divided into four parts.

# 1946

## The United Nations

**January 10, London, England**   Today the United Nations is holding its first meeting. The Foreign Minister from Belgium, Paul Henri Spaak, will be the President of the United Nations. He was elected by one vote. The United States and the countries in the West voted for him. The USSR and the countries of the East wanted a different President. The countries of the West and East do not trust each other. This is very different to when they were Allies in the war.

## Nazi leaders put on trial

**September 30, Nuremberg, Germany**   The wartime Allies have put the Nazi leaders on trial. The trial is being held in Nuremberg, Germany. Eleven Nazi leaders have been sentenced to death. Eight will be put in prison.

## Goering escapes hanging

**October 16, Nuremberg, Germany** Ten Nazi leaders were hanged this morning. But one of the leaders, Hermann Goering, escaped hanging. He killed himself by eating a poisonous pill.

△ Nazi leaders on trial at Nuremberg

# Iron Curtain falls

**March 5, Fulton, USA** The countries of the East and the West are separating into two groups. These groups are often called 'blocs'. The Eastern bloc is controlled by the Communist government in the USSR. Eastern bloc countries include the USSR, Hungary Bulgaria, Romania, Poland, Czechoslovakia, Yugoslavia and the eastern part of Germany (see map). The East and West do not trust each other. Sir Winston Churchill has described the division between the two blocs as an 'Iron Curtain'.

> "A shadow has fallen upon the scenes so lately lighted by the Allied victory . . . From Stettin on the Baltic to Trieste on the Adriatic, an iron curtain has descended across Europe."

### EUROPE IN 1946: THE COMMUNIST BLOC

FINLAND

NORWAY  SWEDEN

North Sea

DENMARK

EIRE

USSR

UNITED KINGDOM

NETH.

GERMANY  POLAND

BELGIUM

CZECHOSLOVAKIA

FRANCE  SWITZ.  AUSTRIA

HUNGARY

ROMANIA

YUGOSLAVIA

SPAIN

ITALY

BULGARIA

Mediterranean Sea

0  km  250

— The 'Iron Curtain'
▢ Communist Bloc in 1946

# The United Nations bans the bomb

**December 14, New York, USA** All the members of the United Nations have voted to ban the atomic bomb. The United Nations want to prevent another atomic explosion like the ones at Hiroshima and Nagasaki.

▽ An atomic explosion

# PEOPLE OF THE 30s AND 40s

## Neville Chamberlain 1869–1940

Neville Chamberlain was the British Prime Minister when Britain entered the war in 1939. Chamberlain tried to persuade Hitler not to go to war. But Hitler fooled Chamberlain with his promises about Czechoslovakia (see page 18). In 1940, Chamberlain resigned and Winston Churchill took his place as Prime Minister. Chamberlain died of cancer in 1940.

## Franklin D. Roosevelt 1882–1945

Franklin D. Roosevelt was President of the United States from 1933 to 1945. He led the United States into World War II in 1941. In 1944 he was elected President for the fourth time. He died in 1945, just before the war ended.

## Walt Disney 1901–1966

Walt Disney was an American film-maker. Many of his films were cartoons. He invented Mickey Mouse, Minnie Mouse, Donald Duck, Goofy, Pluto and many other characters.

## Francisco Franco 1892–1975

Francisco Franco was the leader of Spain from 1937 until 1975. He organised the attack on the government which started the Spanish Civil War.

## Adolf Hitler 1889–1945

Adolf Hitler was born in Austria, but he moved to Germany. He became leader of Germany in 1933. He ordered the invasions of Czechoslovakia, Austria and Poland. World War II followed. He killed himself in 1945, as the Russians entered Berlin.

## Benito Mussolini 1883–1945

Benito Mussolini was the leader of Italy. Before this Mussolini was a teacher, then a journalist. He was on Hitler's side in World War II. But the Allies beat him in 1943. Mussolini was shot and killed in 1945.

## Joseph Stalin 1879–1953

Joseph Stalin was the leader of the revolution in Russia in 1917. Millions of people died on his orders. In World War II, Stalin led Russia to victory over the Germans.

## Winston Churchill 1874–1965

As a young man Winston Churchill was a soldier. He became a member of parliament in 1900. He was in the government during World War I. Churchill became unpopular after the war. This was because he kept giving warnings about the dangers of Communism and of Nazi Germany. He became the British Prime Minister in 1940. He led the British to victory in World War II. He wrote many books and won the Nobel Prize for Literature in 1953.

## Charles de Gaulle 1890–1970

Charles de Gaulle escaped to England when the Germans captured France in 1940. From London he organised the French Resistance against the Germans. After the war he became the French President.

## Viscount Montgomery 1887–1976

Viscount Montgomery's nickname was 'Monty'. He fought in World War I. In World War II he commanded troops in France and in Africa. He planned the battle of El Alamein against the German army. This battle ended with a victory for the Allies. It was an important turning point in the war. After this the Allies were able to advance on the Germans in North Africa.

# Glossary

**abdicate**: to give up something formally, for example a throne.

**Abyssinia**: a country in northeast Africa now called Ethiopia.

**air raid**: an attack by enemy planes. The planes often dropped bombs.

**the Allies**: the countries that fought against Germany and Japan in World War II. The main Allied countries were Britain and the Commonwealth countries, the USA, Russia, France, China and Poland.

**atomic bomb**: a powerful bomb that causes much death and destruction.

**Communists**: Communists believe that all property and industry in a country should belong to the state.

**concentration camps**: camps built by the Nazis. The Nazis put their enemies in these camps. Millions of people died in concentration camps.

**ghetto**: in World War II an area of a city in which Jewish people were forced to live.

**Luftwaffe**: the German airforce. 'Luftwaffe' means 'air weapon'.

**Nazi**: the short name in German for 'The National Socialist German Worker's Party'.

**Reichstag**: the German parliament and the building it met in.

**Resistance**: in France the secret organisation that fought the Germans while the country was occupied.

**treaty**: an agreement between two or more countries.

# Index

# Sociology in Pictures
## Research Methods

# Michael Haralambos
### with Wendy Hope

### Illustrated by Matt Timson

## Contents

**Published by Collins Educational**

An imprint of HarperCollins Publishers, 77-85 Fulham Palace Road, Hammersmith, London W6 8JB

© Michael Haralambos, 2012

10 9 8 7 6 5 4 3 2 1

ISBN 978-0-00-748193-4

Michael Haralambos asserts his moral rights to be identified as the author of this work.

British Library Cataloguing in Publication Data.
A catalogue record for this publication is available from the British Library.

**Typography and design** by John A Collins

**Printed and bound** in the UK by www.waringcollins.com

**Thanks** To Peter Langley who, with Michael Haralambos, developed the idea of sociology in pictures. And thanks to Catherine Steers and Kimberley Atkins at Collins Educational for their support.

**Note** In many cases, the speech bubbles are direct quotes or paraphrases from actual research.

**Dedication** To Charlie, Sammy, Max, Miles, Isabelle, Lottie and Woody

# PARTICIPANT OBSERVATION

Participant observation is a research method which involves the researcher taking part in the activities of those they are studying.

## HANGING OUT

Sudhir Venkatesh studied the Black Kings, an African-American gang who sold crack in Chicago. He began with a questionnaire survey which he quickly replaced with participant observation (Venkatesh, 2009).

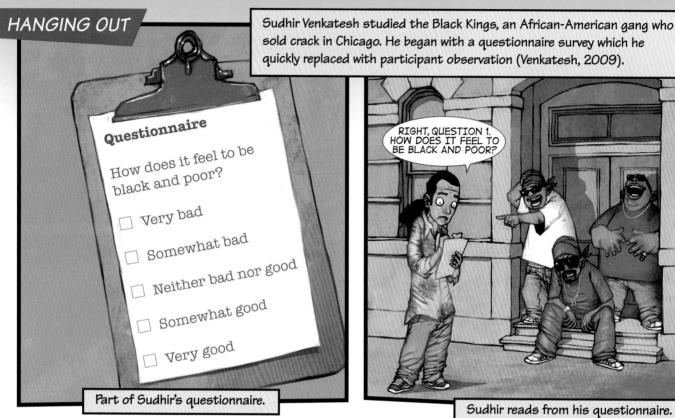

Part of Sudhir's questionnaire.

RIGHT, QUESTION 1. HOW DOES IT FEEL TO BE BLACK AND POOR?

Sudhir reads from his questionnaire.

YOU AIN'T GOING TO LEARN SHIT WITH THIS! WITH PEOPLE LIKE US YOU SHOULD HANG OUT AND GET TO KNOW WHAT WE DO.

JT the gang leader gives Sudhir some advice.

LOOK, LISTEN AND STAY IN THE BACKGROUND.

'I took JT's advice and hung out with the gang. They didn't like interview questions. They probably had enough of that from cops and social workers. So I just made small talk. In general, I said very little.'

# GAINING ENTRY

One of the difficulties of participant observation is gaining entry into the group. It helps if important members are on your side.

**DAY 1**

**DAY 2**

**DAY 3**

# ACTING NORMALLY

Researchers want to observe people behaving normally. They do their best not to influence those they observe. This can be seen from research by David Hargreaves (1967), who studied teachers and students in a boys' secondary school in northern England. For part of his research, he sat at the back of the classroom and observed what was going on.

DAY 1

DAY 5

TURN AROUND AND PAY ATTENTION, BOYS.

'At first my presence caused changes in the boys' behaviour. But once the boys got used to me, they behaved normally.'

THE TEACHERS PUT ON A SHOW FOR YOU – SMILES AND ALL THAT.

IF YOU WEREN'T THERE, MR O WOULD GET REAL MAD.

WHEN YOU'RE IN HE TRIED TO ACT CALMLY AS THOUGH HE'S A LITTLE ANGEL.

'Many of the teachers appeared to behave quite naturally and act as if I was not in the room at all. But it is difficult to check on the extent of the changes my presence produced.'

# STREET CORNER SOCIETY

In 1937, William Foote Whyte began a 3½ year study of an Italian-American gang in Boston. Based on participant observation, this classic study was called *Street Corner Society*.

'As I sat and listened, I learned the answers to questions I would not have had the sense to ask if I had been getting my information solely on an interviewing basis' (Whyte, 1943).

'The gambler's jaw dropped. He glared at me. For the rest of that evening I felt very uncomfortable.'

Next day, Doc the gang leader, said, 'Go easy on that who, what, why, when stuff Bill. You ask those questions and people will clam up on you.'

Doc worked closely with Bill. 'Now, when I do something, I have to think what Bill Whyte would want to know about it and how I can explain it. Before, I used to do things by instinct.'

# OBSERVATIONS IN CONTEXT

Participant observers look at what people do in their normal, everyday settings, how they make sense of their experiences and how they act in different situations.

## FIDDLING

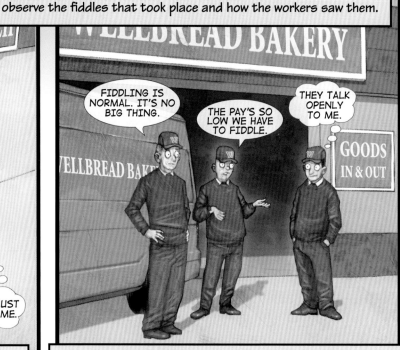

Jason Ditton (1977) worked for over a year in a bakery in order to observe the fiddles that took place and how the workers saw them.

Fiddles are seen as 'perks' rather than a crime.

Salesmen justify stealing bread and overcharging customers.

## MANLY FLAWS

Elliot Liebow (1967) spent 1½ years observing African-American men in Washington D.C. The men were either on welfare or in low-paid jobs. Their income was insufficient to support a wife and family. Most had failed marriages.

Failure as a husband is explained by being a man. Boasting about 'manly flaws' helps to restore self-respect, but it does not always prevent the pain of a broken marriage from finding expression.

# ETHNOGRAPHY

Ethnography is the study of the way of life of a group of people. It aims to see their world from their perspective. Ethnographers argue that the best way to do this is to immerse yourself in their everyday life using participant observation as the main research method.

Bronislaw Malinowski (1884-1942) was one of the founding fathers of ethnography. He spent two years living with the Trobriand Islanders in the Western Pacific.

I'M HERE TO STUDY YOUR WAY OF LIFE.

THE GARDEN MAGICIAN WILL GIVE ME A GOOD CROP

The aim of ethnography is to 'grasp the native's point of view... to realise his vision of his world' (Malinowski, 1922).

Trobriand men spend half their lives gardening. The garden magician conducts ceremonies to help the crops grow.

THAT'S A FINE YAM HARVEST.

I FEEL REALLY PROUD. PEOPLE WILL LOOK UP TO ME.

WELL DONE.

MY JOB IS TO SEE GARDENING THROUGH THEIR EYES.

At harvest time men display their crops. People walk from garden to garden admiring the best crops and praising the best gardeners.

# TYPES OF INTERVIEW

## STRUCTURED INTERVIEW

This is a structured interview – it is a questionnaire read out to the interviewee.

## UNSTRUCTURED INTERVIEW

This is an unstructured interview – it is less directed and more like a conversation.

## RAPPORT

Interviewers are often advised to establish rapport – a warm and friendly relationship with the interviewee.

## ASSERTIVENESS

Howard Becker (1971) sometimes used a more assertive approach which may lead people to be 'considerably more frank than they had originally intended'.

## FEMINIST INTERVIEWING

Some feminists argue that interviews should be woman to woman. The interviewer should express sympathy and understanding based on shared experience and treat the interviewee as an equal.

# INTERVIEW EFFECTS

Interviews can be influenced by the age, gender, status, ethnicity and social class of the interviewer and the interviewee, by the way they see each other and by the setting in which the interview takes place.

## DEFINING THE INTERVIEWER

In a study of organisational culture, Martin Parker (2000) found that interviewees defined him in different ways. These definitions influenced the answers they gave.

# SOCIAL DESIRABILITY EFFECTS

People tend to present themselves in the best possible light in interviews. This can lead to an emphasis on socially desirable aspects of their behaviour.

## GOING TO CHURCH

A survey conducted by Gallup found that 35% of Episcopalians in the USA said that they had been to church in the last 7 days. Yet figures from the churches showed that only 16% actually did so (Bruce, 1995).

## TAKING COCAINE

Over 600 Chicago residents were asked if they had taken cocaine in the last year. After the interview, 571 agreed to take a drugs test. Around three-quarters of those testing positive for cocaine use did *not* report taking it (Johnson et al, 2002).

# INTERVIEWS IN CONTEXT

The following interviews were used to assess the linguistic skills of African-American boys (Labov, 1973). The boys were asked to describe a toy plane.

## INTERVIEW 1

The boy sees the interview as threatening. He gives short answers followed by long silences.

## INTERVIEW 2

This time the interviewer is black but the boy's responses are similar to those in Interview 1.

## INTERVIEW 3

The interviewer and the boy are the same as in Interview 2. The setting is more informal, the boy's best friend is present and they are supplied with crisps. The boy is now confident, talkative and gives a detailed description of the plane.

# QUESTIONNAIRES

## CONSTRUCTING A QUESTIONNAIRE

Questionnaires are lists of questions. They should be clear and straightforward and mean the same thing to everybody who answers them. Here are some of the dos and don'ts of questionnaires.

## AVOID OVERSIMPLIFICATION

## AVOID LEADING QUESTIONS

## BE SPECIFIC

## KEEP THE LANGUAGE SIMPLE

## AVOID EMOTIVE LANGUAGE

## KEEP IT SHORT

# ANSWERING QUESTIONS

When answering questions, people sometimes say one thing and do another. And sometimes they say things they believe to be true which are not actually true.

## YES AND NO

In the 1930s, a young Chinese couple visited 250 hotels and restaurants in the USA. Only once were they refused service. Letters were sent to the places they visited asking would they accept Chinese guests. 92% said 'no', 7% 'uncertain' and 1% 'yes' (LaPiere, 1934).

## FALSE MEMORIES

In a study of memory, 36% of adult Americans recalled a childhood meeting with Bugs Bunny at Disneyland. This could not have happened since Bugs Bunny is not a Disney character (Loftus, 2003).

Children were given a list of horror videos, some with fictitious titles such as *Blood On The Teeth Of The Vampire*. 68% claimed to have seen one or more of the fictitious films (Cumberbatch, 1994).

# SAMPLING METHODS

A social survey involves the collection of the same type of data from a fairly large number of people. Social surveys are usually based on samples drawn from the group to be studied – for example, a sample of young people or a sample of women. The data usually comes from questionnaires or from structured interviews.

## REPRESENTATIVE SAMPLES

**Families with dependent children**

Married and cohabiting couples 5.6 million (74%)

Lone mothers 1.8 million (24%)

Lone fathers 0.2 million (2%)

I WANT MY SAMPLE TO HAVE THE SAME PROPORTION OF FAMILY TYPES WITH DEPENDENT CHILDREN AS THE POPULATION AS A WHOLE.

Ideally samples should be representative – they should reflect the group as a whole. If the sample is representative, then the findings of the survey are more likely to apply to the wider society.

## SIMPLE RANDOM SAMPLES

I WANT EACH MEMBER OF THE SAMPLE TO BE SELECTED BY CHANCE.

The researcher obtains a list of names, such as a register of college students. Every name is given a number and the sample is selected by using a list of random numbers. Simple random samples are not necessarily representative.

## STRATIFIED RANDOM SAMPLES

I THINK AGE IS AN IMPORTANT FACTOR IN INTERNET USE. MY SAMPLE MUST REFLECT DIFFERENT AGE GROUPS.

A stratified random sample reflects the population as a whole in terms of different groups or strata, such as age or ethnic groups. The sample is randomly selected from one or more of these groups.

## QUOTA SAMPLES

A quota sample is like a stratified random sample but the selection is not random. The researcher just fills their quota – e.g., 20 men and 20 women – with the first available people.

## SNOWBALL SAMPLES

A snowball sample builds up like rolling a snowball. The researcher finds one person to fit the sample, that person finds another and so on. This is useful when people do not want to be identified or are difficult to find – e.g., criminals, drug addicts and sex workers. Snowball sampling is unlikely to produce a representative sample.

## VOLUNTEER SAMPLES

Volunteer samples are drawn from people responding to adverts. Those who volunteer may have a particular reason for doing so – they may have a strongly held point of view or a grievance to express. This may result in an unrepresentative sample.

# RESPONSE RATES

The response rate is the percentage of the sample that participates in the research. A low response rate can lead to an unrepresentative sample. Those who don't participate may be significantly different from those who do.

Postal questionnaires often have a low response rate. Responders tend to be better educated than non-responders.

Response is more likely if the researcher drops off and picks up the questionnaire and explains the research.

Language difficulties can lead to low response rates.

The subject matter can affect the response rate. In one study, 19% of the sample refused to participate when they found that it was about incest (Russell, 1986).

Many families refused to participate in the Department of Health study of children's weight. Those with overweight children were more likely to refuse (Bryman, 2008).

Only 61% of a sample of 2,000 offenders agreed to take part in a Home Office survey of probation. The non-responders may have had more negative experiences of probation (Mair, 2000).

A longitudinal study looks at the same group of people over a period of time. The National Child Development Study in Britain began with a sample of 17,400 newborn children in 1958. By 2008, the sample, now aged 50, was down to 9,790 due to death, emigration, failure to trace and refusal to participate. This probably resulted in a less representative sample (ESDS, 2011).

# TYPES OF DATA

Data is the information used in research. There are two main types of data – quantitative and qualitative data.

## QUANTITATIVE DATA

Quantitative data are data in the form of numbers.

In 1971 in the UK there were 205,000 women in higher education, 33% of all higher education students. In 2008/09 there were 1,451,000 women, nearly 60% of all higher education students (*Social Trends*, 2011).

In Britain in 1998, 30% of men smoked cigarettes, in 2009, 22%. For women, 26% smoked in 1998, 20% in 2009 (*Social Trends*, 2011).

In England and Wales there were 352,000 marriages in 1981 and 231,490 in 2009 (*Social Trends*, 2011).

Qualitative data are all types of data that are not in the form of numbers. They include data from observations and interviews, from written sources such as diaries and newspapers, and from pictorial sources such as paintings and posters.

Gathering qualitative data from observations of fans at a football match.

Collecting qualitative data from a discussion after the match.

Taking notes during an in-depth interview with a fan.

# EXPERIMENTS

## LABORATORY EXPERIMENTS

This laboratory experiment tests the statement that noise has an effect on memory.

Participants are asked to recall a list of words. Some are placed in a quiet room, others with loud music. Everything else is the same. If there are differences in recall between the two groups, this suggests that noise affects memory.

Laboratory experiments have been criticised as artificial. If so, they may not reflect behaviour in the 'real' world.

## FIELD EXPERIMENTS

Field experiments take place in normal, everyday settings.

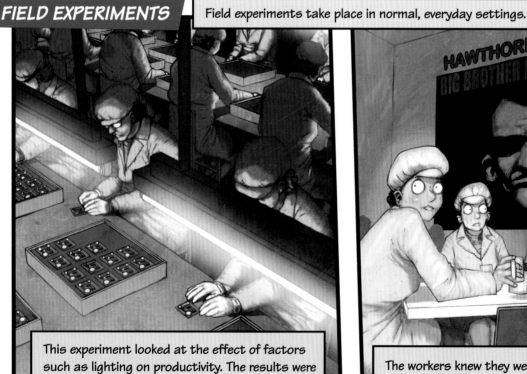

This experiment looked at the effect of factors such as lighting on productivity. The results were confusing. For example, productivity increased whether lighting was increased or decreased.

The workers knew they were being observed – this is what affected their productivity. This is known as the Hawthorne effect.

# CORRELATION

If two things are correlated, then they increase and decrease together, or when one increases, the other decreases. This may be due to one causing the other, to a third factor which causes both, or due to chance.

## CHANCE

In Copenhagen for the 12 years following World War Two, the number of storks nesting in the city and the number of human babies born went up and down together. This correlation is probably a coincidence – due to chance.

## A THIRD FACTOR

There is a correlation between yellow grass and the sale of cold drinks. The yellower the grass, the more cold drinks are sold. This correlation is probably due to a third factor – the temperature.

# TESTING HYPOTHESES

An hypothesis is an expected relationship between two or more factors. It is designed to be tested against evidence. Experiments are often used to test hypotheses. Hypotheses are often drawn from theories.

The self-fulfilling prophecy theory states that someone's expectations of another person will tend to influence that person's behaviour.

Robert Rosenthal and Leonora Jacobson (1968) designed an experiment to test the hypothesis that teachers' expectations of children's ability will affect their progress. They began by giving an IQ test to primary school pupils.

The researchers gave the teachers false information. The names on the list were a random sample of pupils, NOT those with the highest scores.

The pupils were given a second IQ test 8 months after the first. In general, those on the list made greater gains in IQ.

The results of the experiment appeared to support the researchers' hypothesis. Later experiments have produced similar results but others have not.

# MULTIPLE CAUSES

Often events are caused by a number of things – they have multiple causes. This can be seen from the dramatic decline of crime in the USA in the 1990s and the early 2000s.

## ZERO TOLERANCE POLICING

In 1994, zero tolerance policing began in New York – the police clamped down on all crimes, however small. Within 2 years, murder was halved and robberies were down by a third (Chaundary and Walker, 1996).

## VARIOUS FACTORS

The US economy grew and unemployment fell between 1992 and the mid-2000s. The age group with the highest crime risk (15-29) dropped from 27.4% of the population in 1980 to 20.9% in 2000. Police numbers increased by 14% in the 1990s (Zimring, 2007).

## PRISON

The US prison population grew from 500,000 in 1980 to 2.4 million in 2011.

## GUN CONTROL

There were sharp falls in handgun homicides in cities like Washington D.C. with strict gun control laws. But there were also sharp falls in cities like Houston where it was easy to buy guns (McGreal, 2011).

## CRACK COCAINE

The crack epidemic saw a rise in violent crime as rival gangs fought to control the trade and addicts robbed to feed their habit. The demand for crack declined from the mid-1990s as did violent crime (McGreal, 2011).

## TARGET HARDENING

Target hardening – for example, surveillance and electronic security – has made it increasingly difficult to break into buildings and vehicles (McGreal, 2011).

# CASE STUDIES

A case study is a detailed study of one particular case or instance of something – for example, a study of an individual, group or community.

## LIFE HISTORIES

A life history is a case study of a particular individual – their life as they see it – taken from a series of in-depth interviews.

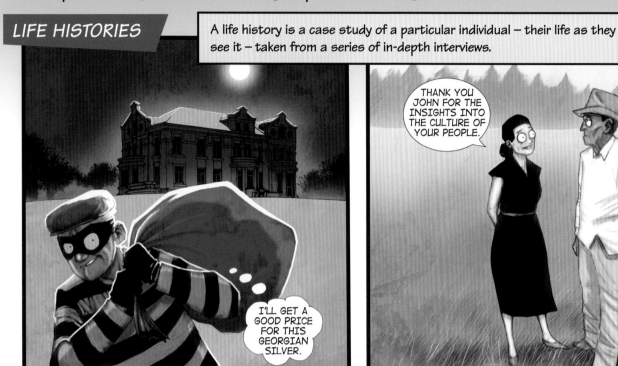

Mike Maguire (2000) obtained the life history of a 'specialist country house burglar'. The life history method allowed him to 'probe much more deeply than one-off interviews'.

Margot Liberty obtained the life history of John Stands In Timber, one of the last Cheyenne to recall their traditional way of life. 'His kind of inside view will never be achieved again' (Stands In Timber and Liberty, 1967).

## A COMMUNITY

Paul Heelas and Linda Woodhead (2005) used Kendal, a town of around 28,000 in the Lake District, for a detailed case study of spirituality and religion. They found a rise in spirituality and a decline in religion. However it is not possible to make generalisations from a single case study.

## A SOCIAL MOVEMENT

When Prophecy Fails (Festinger et al, 2011) is a case study of a small social movement, The Seekers, who prophesied a catastrophic flood. Those who joined the movement would be saved from the deluge.

MESSAGES FROM THE GUARDIANS ON PLANET CLARION

DECEMBER 21ST THE GREAT FLOOD

RESCUED BY FLYING SAUCERS

Mrs Marian Keech, a suburban housewife in the USA, claimed to have received messages from outer space about a devastating flood due on December 21st.

**DECEMBER 21ST**

NOTHING'S HAPPENED!

WHERE IS THE FLOOD?

I CAN'T BELIEVE IT.

ON AIR

KRON TV

THE GOD OF EARTH STOPPED THE FLOOD. WE AWAIT MESSAGES FROM THE GUARDIANS. THEY STILL CARE FOR US.

Case studies show that no two social situations are the same. However, they sometimes show that similar situations produce similar results – as in this case, when prophecy fails people often cling to their beliefs.

# LONGITUDINAL STUDIES

Longitudinal studies are designed to study development and change. They examine the same group of people over fairly long periods of time.

The National Child Development Study began with over 17,400 babies born in Britain in March 1958. Here are some of its findings on social inequality.

## UPPER CLASS

1958 FATHER – LAWYER

1979 SON – UNIVERSITY DEGREE

1990 WELL – PAID JOB

2000 OWN HOUSE

2004 TRANSPORT

The class you are born into can have a powerful effect on your life. In general, the higher your class of birth the more likely you are to live a long and healthy life, to have a high income and a high living standard (Elliott and Vaitilingam, 2008).

## LOWER CLASS

1958 FATHER – LABOURER

1979 SON – NO QUALIFICATIONS

1990 UNEMPLOYED

Job Centre

2000 RENTED FLAT

2004 TRANSPORT

Starting with a sample of 1,125 young people aged 14 in Merseyside and Greater Manchester, the North West Longitudinal Study tracked them for one or more years from 1991 to 1995. Each year they were given a questionnaire about their attitudes to and use of drugs. The findings were very different from the picture presented by parts of the media and many politicians (Parker et al, 1998).

Tabloid press.

House of Commons.

There was little evidence of pressure from friends to take drugs.

Most drug users were fairly conventional with no criminal record.

By age 18, 59% had tried cannabis, 20% ecstasy, 10% heroin, 6% cocaine.

Many young people saw the occasional and sometimes regular use of 'soft' drugs as a normal part of their recreation.

# OFFICIAL STATISTICS

Official statistics are numerical data produced by national and local government bodies. They can be compiled and used in various ways.

## CRIME STATISTICS

Official police crime statistics are based on crimes recorded by the police. They can be affected by the priorities of different police forces.

The annual British Crime Survey asks people if they have been the victim of crimes. In 2010/11 it was based on 46,000 interviews in England and Wales (Fitzpatrick and Grant, 2011).

## POLITICS AND STATISTICS

Conservative governments changed the method for counting unemployment over 30 times between 1982 and 1992. In nearly every case this led to a drop in the official unemployment figures (Denscombe, 1994).

A change in the methods of police recording resulted in a rise in the official rate of violent crime (UK Statistics Authority, 2010).

# STATISTICS ARE IMPORTANT

*Reading the Riots* is a study based on in-depth interviews with 270 people who took part in the August 2011 riots in England (Guardian, 2011). It found that hostility towards the police was a major reason for the riots. Official statistics on stop and search help to explain this hostility.

## STOP AND SEARCH

In England and Wales in 2009/10 black people were seven times more likely to be stopped and searched by the police than white people (Ministry of Justice, 2011). In *Reading the Riots*, 73% of interviewees said they had been stopped and searched in the last year, 71% said more than once (50% of the interviewees were black).

## REVENGE

Many saw the riots as revenge for the way police conducted stop and search – for the humiliation, unjust suspicion and discrimination they experienced. (Speech bubbles taken from *Reading the Riots*.)

# DOCUMENTS

Documents refer to a wide range of written and recorded material. John Scott (1990) suggest four ways of assessing documents – authenticity, credibility, representativeness and meaning.

## AUTHENTICITY

Is the document genuine?

In 1983, the German magazine *Stern* announced that it had acquired Hitler's diaries – 62 handwritten volumes for which it paid $4 million. Research later showed that the diaries were forgeries.

## CREDIBILITY

Does the document provide a true picture or does it distort events?

THIS WILL SET THE RECORD STRAIGHT.

Former US president George W. Bush was strongly criticised for authorising 'waterboarding' – a form of torture – for al Qaeda suspects. He claimed in his memoirs that this saved lives. According to British officials, there is no evidence to support this claim.

## REPRESENTATIVENESS

Is the document typical or a one-off?

Newspaper headlines

1898 **The avalanche of brutality under the name of Hooliganism** *(Daily Graphic)*

1931 **Street gangs – this greatest menace of the century** *(Reynolds News)*

1955 **War on Teddy Boys – menace in the streets of Britain** *(Daily Dispatch)*

2005 **Yobs are intimidating entire neighbourhoods** *(Daily Mail)*

From the 1800s to the present day, reports in tabloid newspapers have often pictured young men as 'ruffians', 'hooligans' and 'yobs' (Pearson, 1983).

An image of Teddy Boys based on newspaper reports from the 1950s.

What does the document mean to those who produced it, to the people who see or hear it and to the researcher who interprets it?

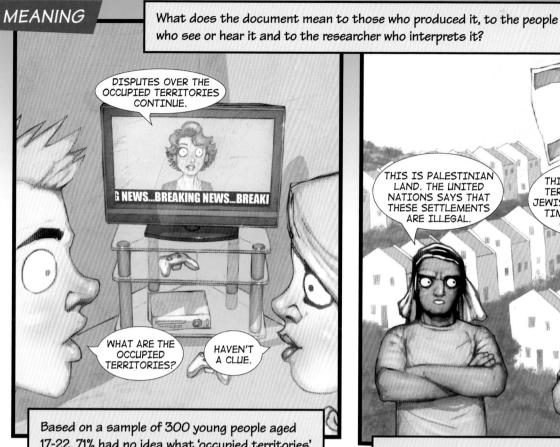

DISPUTES OVER THE OCCUPIED TERRITORIES CONTINUE.

G NEWS...BREAKING NEWS...BREAKI

WHAT ARE THE OCCUPIED TERRITORIES?

HAVEN'T A CLUE.

Based on a sample of 300 young people aged 17-22, 71% had no idea what 'occupied territories' meant, 11% thought it was Palestinians occupying Israeli land and only 9% got it right – Israelis occupying Palestinian land (Philo and Miller, 2002).

THIS IS PALESTINIAN LAND. THE UNITED NATIONS SAYS THAT THESE SETTLEMENTS ARE ILLEGAL.

THIS IS NOT OCCUPIED TERRITORY. THIS WAS JEWISH LAND IN BIBLICAL TIMES. IT IS PART OF OUR HOMELAND.

An Israeli settlement on the West Bank, part of the territory occupied by Israel after the Six-Day War in 1967. Comments based on videos shown on YouTube.

'I check cheddar like a food inspector' (from *Public Service Announcement*).

**'check' means to collect, 'cheddar' means money.**

'I'm out here slingin' (from *Coming of Age*)

**'slingin' means selling drugs.**

'Can't blow too hard, life's a deck of cards' (from *Fallin'*).

**'Can't blow too hard' means 'you can't show off too much or your whole life can tumble'.**

Jay-Z translates lines from his songs – taken from his book *Decoded* (2010).

## EXCHANGING NOTES

Valerie Hey (1997) studied girls' friendship patterns in two London comprehensive schools. Part of her data came from notes the girls exchanged during their lessons.

15 notes were exchanged between 3 girls in a history lesson. 90% of what they wrote concerned their relations with each other.

One teacher retrieved discarded notes from her waste basket. Other notes were picked up by Valerie Hey who scrabbled around the floor after lessons.

Valerie Hey was concerned about the ethics of collecting private and personal notes without permission.

# RELIABILITY AND VALIDITY

If different researchers using the same methods obtain the same results, then the methods and the results are reliable. But this does not necessarily mean they give a true or valid picture. Nor does it mean that the conclusions drawn from the data are valid.

EVERY MORNING THE SUN COMES UP IN THE SAME PLACE, MOVES ACROSS THE SKY AND GOES DOWN ON THE OTHER SIDE. CLEARLY, THE SUN GOES ROUND THE EARTH.

The observations are reliable – everybody observes the same thing. But the conclusion is not valid – the sun does NOT go round the earth.

STOP NOW!

BUT I'VE NOT FINISHED

Yakima Native American children got low scores on IQ tests because they did not finish in time. Yakima culture placed little importance on speed. The tests were not a valid measure of their intelligence – they mainly reflected the children's culture (Klineberg, 1971).

## REDFIELD'S OBSERVATIONS

## LEWIS'S OBSERVATIONS

In the late 1920s, Robert Redfield (1930) studied the village of Tepoztlan in Mexico. He found a close-knit, harmonious and happy community. Oscar Lewis (1951) studied the same village 17 years later. He saw the community as divided by envy, distrust and conflict. Redfield and Lewis believed the main reason for these differences resulted from differences between them in terms of their outlook and personality. If so, their observations were not reliable. Nor were they valid – at best they were one-sided.

# SOCIAL FACTS

Social facts are aspects of society which direct people's behaviour. They can be social relationships like marriage or social institutions like religion.

## DURKHEIM AND SUICIDE

Emile Durkheim looked at two social facts – the level of social integration and the rate of suicide. He argued that the greater the level of social integration the lower the level of suicide. In highly integrated groups control over behaviour is strong and there will be considerable pressure against suicide.

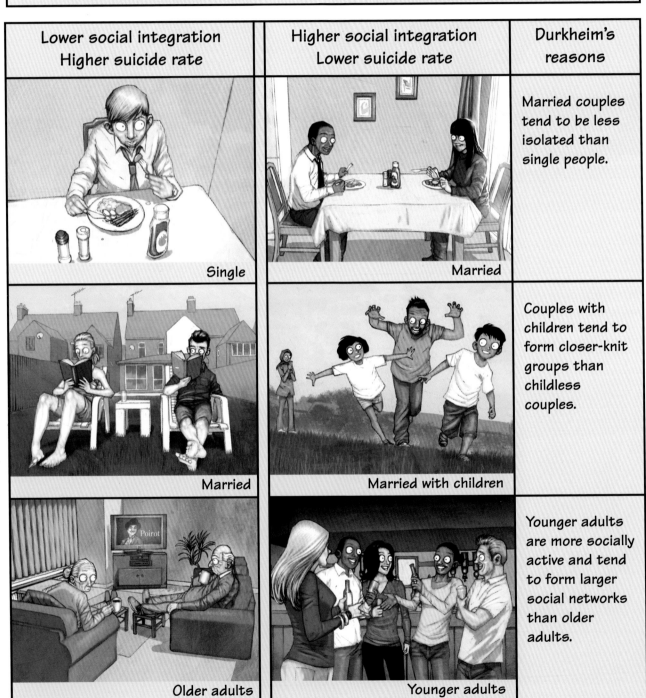

| Lower social integration Higher suicide rate | Higher social integration Lower suicide rate | Durkheim's reasons |
|---|---|---|
| Single | Married | Married couples tend to be less isolated than single people. |
| Married | Married with children | Couples with children tend to form closer-knit groups than childless couples. |
| Older adults | Younger adults | Younger adults are more socially active and tend to form larger social networks than older adults. |

| Lower social integration Higher suicide rate | Higher social integration Lower suicide rate | Durkheim's reasons |
|---|---|---|
| City dwellers | Country dwellers | Village communities are likely to be more integrated than urban areas. |
| Protestants | Catholics | Catholicism integrates its members more strongly into a religious community. |
| Peace | War | By identifying a common enemy, war is more likely to unify a nation than peace. |

# SOCIAL CONSTRUCTION

The idea of social construction provides an alternative to social facts. It argues that people construct meanings which form social reality. The job of the sociologist is to discover these meanings. So, when studying suicide, sociologists should discover the meanings used to categorise deaths as suicide.

In *Discovering Suicide*, J. Maxwell Atkinson (1978) argues that coroners have a 'commonsense theory of suicide' which includes a 'typical suicide biography' and a 'typical suicide death'. The nearer a death fits this theory, the more likely it will be defined as suicide.

# POSITIVISM AND INTERPRETIVISM

Some sociologists identify two main approaches to research – positivism and interpretivism. Others reject this distinction, saying there are many different approaches.

## POSITIVISM

Positivism focuses on social facts, on quantitative data and cause and effect relationships.

I'VE BEEN CALLED A POSITIVIST BECAUSE I LIKE TO MEASURE THINGS AND I LIKE MY DATA IN NUMBERS.

I LIKE QUESTIONNAIRES AND SOCIAL SURVEYS BASED ON REPRESENTATIVE SAMPLES.

I WANT TO FIND CORRELATIONS BETWEEN SOCIAL FACTS WHICH INDICATE CAUSAL RELATIONSHIPS.

## INTERPRETIVISM

Interpretivism focuses on interpreting the meanings which are seen to direct human action. It favours qualitative data.

Coroner's Court

WHAT ARE THE MEANINGS HE USES TO DEFINE SUICIDE?

CAN YOU DESCRIBE A TYPICAL SUICIDE DEATH?

DROWNING, DRUG OVERDOSE, HANGING, GASSING.

J.Maxwell Atkinson used observation and in-depth interviews in his research on suicide.

DO I HAVE TO CHOOSE?

Many sociologists use a variety of research methods and both quantitative and qualitative data.

Starting research involves thinking of a topic to study and deciding what methods to use to collect the information.

Sociologists choose a research topic that interests them and that they think is important.

Researchers often begin in the library, reading studies on their chosen topic.

Research in schools serving Jamie Oliver's 'healthy meals' showed improvements in Key Stage 2 test results and a 15% drop in absences due to illness (Belot and James, 2009).

The British Sociological Association's ethical guidelines state that people should be made aware that they are participating in research.

I'll join in and observe the kitchen staff and pupils.

I'll interview the school cook, the head teacher and the local authority school meals' superviser.

I'll design a simple questionnaire for 7 to 11 year old pupils.

I'll try and get some parents to take part in a discussion on school meals.

# CHOOSING A TOPIC

There are many reasons for choosing a particular research topic. Here are a few.

## VALUES

Ann Oakley, a feminist, wanted to bring women's issues centre stage. Her male colleagues in the 1960s were puzzled that she chose to study something as 'insignificant' as housework.

## MORALITY

Peter Townsend (1928-2009) was driven by his convictions. He spent over 50 years researching poverty and campaigning on behalf of the poor.

## ISSUES

Choosing a research topic is influenced by the issues of the day, for example, globalisation.

## FUNDING

The choice of topic may be influenced by the priorities of the funding organisations.

# MIXED METHODS

A mixed method approach combines qualitative and quantitative methods, for instance, participant observation and questionnaires. It aims to get the best of both worlds. The example of mixed methods below is taken from *Goth: Identity, Style and Subculture* (2002) by Paul Hodkinson. He had been a Goth for ten years when he conducted the research.

## PARTICIPANT OBSERVATION

Participant observation at the Whitby Gothic Weekend. This festival is 'the ultimate experience in taking part in the Goth scene'.

## QUESTIONNAIRES

'The questionnaires provided useful quantitative data and some extremely valuable comments.'

## INTERVIEWS

The conversation in the interviews was 'open and flowing'. They provided 'in-depth, quality information'.

# TRIANGULATION

Like mixed methods, triangulation is a research design which uses a variety of methods. It can also involve a number of different researchers. Triangulation aims to 1) provide a more complete and rounded picture and 2) check on the validity of research findings.

The following example of triangulation was used by Sandra Walklate and her research team in a study of the fear of crime in two high crime urban areas in northern England (Walklate, 2000).

SOCIOLOGY DEPARTMENT

The research team. Being an all-women team may have been an advantage – 'we posed no threat'.

Getting to know the research area with the help of police officers.

Going to pubs and chatting to locals.

CRIME RATE

In-depth interviews with professionals such as social workers and probation officers who work in the area.

Observing police/community meetings.

Analysis of local newspapers.

Mature students from a local university conducting a house-to-house survey.

Focus group discussions with some of the survey participants.

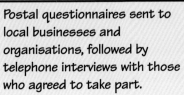

Postal questionnaires sent to local businesses and organisations, followed by telephone interviews with those who agreed to take part.

Talking about triangulation.

# RESEARCH ETHICS

Research ethics are the moral guidelines for researchers. Participants must be informed about the research, they must not be deceived, their consent must be given, they have the right to withdraw, they must be protected from discomfort and harm, their privacy should not be invaded and their identity kept secret.

## MILGRAM'S OBEDIENCE EXPERIMENT

The American psychologist Stanley Milgram (1963) conducted an experiment to see how far people would obey commands which they felt were wrong and would harm others. The participants were told that the experiment was a 'scientific study' of the effect of punishment – electric shocks – on learning. Unknown to the participants, the shocks were not real.

The man on the right is an actor. He is pretending to suffer extreme pain.

Yet over 80% of the participants thought that the experiment was worthwhile.

Milgram justifies his research methods: 'This experiment is important. If one man in a white coat can get people to harm others, think what governments can command.'

## THE 'TEAROOM TRADE'

Laud Humphreys (1970) studied casual sex between men in public toilets in the USA. This is known as the 'tearoom trade' in gay slang.

Humphreys acted as a 'watchqueen' warning of the approach of strangers and the police. He kept his identity as a researcher secret.

I'M FROM THE HEALTH SERVICE. THANKS FOR AGREEING TO THIS INTERVIEW.

A year later, Humphreys interviewed some of the men he had observed. The interviews were conducted in their homes. Humphreys changed his appearance and pretended that he was doing a survey on health. He tracked down their names and addresses from their licence plate numbers.

I HAD TO KEEP MY RESEARCH SECRET AND INVADE THE MEN'S PRIVACY IN ORDER TO CONDUCT THE STUDY.

Humphreys defends his methods. His research showed that the participants were not 'dangerous deviants' – most were 'respectable' married men.

# REFERENCES

Atkinson, J.M. (1978). *Discovering suicide*. London: Macmillan.

Becker, H.S. (1971). Social-class variations in the teacher-pupil relationship. In B.R.Cosin et al (eds.), *School and society*. London: Routledge.

Belot, M. & James, J. (2009). *Healthy school meals and educational outcomes*. Colchester: Institute for Social and Economic Research.

Bruce, S. (1995). Religion and the sociology of religion. In M.Haralambos (ed.), *Developments in Sociology, Volume 11*. Ormskirk: Causeway Press.

Bryman, A. (2008). *Social research methods* (3$^{rd}$ edition). Oxford: Oxford University Press.

Chaundhary, V. & Walker, M. (1996). The petty crime war. *The Guardian*, 21.11.1996.

Cumberbatch, G. (1994). Legislating mythology: Video violence and children. *Journal of Mental Health*, 3, 485-494.

Denscombe, M. (1994). *Sociology update*. Leicester: Olympus Books.

Ditton, J. (1977). *Part-time crime: An ethnography of fiddling and pilferage*. London: Macmillan.

Durkheim, E. (1970, originally 1897). *Suicide: A study in sociology*. London: Routledge & Kegan Paul.

Elliot, J. & Vaitilingam, R. (eds.) (2008). *Now we are 50: Key findings from the National Child Development Study, summary report*. London: Institute of Education, University of London.

ESDS (Economic and Social Data Service). (2011). *Guide to the National Child Development Study*.

Festinger, L., Riecken, H.W. & Schachter, S. (2011 edition). *When prophecy fails*. Blacksburg, VA: Wilder Publications.

Fitzpatrick, A. & Grant, C. (2011). *The 2010/11 British Crime Survey: Technical report, Volume 1*. London: Home Office.

Guardian. (2011). *Reading the riots*. Various issue of *The Guardian* 05.12.2011–10.12.2011.

Hargreaves, D.H. (1967). *Social relations in a secondary school*. London: Routledge & Kegan Paul.

Heelas, P. & Woodhead, L. (2005). *The spiritual revolution: Why religion is giving way to spirituality*. Oxford: Blackwell.

Hey, V. (1997). *The company she keeps: An ethnography of girls' friendships*. Buckingham: Open University Press.

Humphreys, L. (1970). *Tearoom trade: Impersonal sex in public places*. London: Duckworth.

Jay-Z. (2010). *Decoded*. London: Virgin Books.

Johnson, T.P. et al (2002). *A validation of the Crowne-Marlowe social desirability scale*. Chicago: Survey Research Laboratory, University of Illinois at Chicago.

Klineberg, O. (1971). Race and IQ. *Courier*, 24, 10.

Labov, W. (1973). The logic of non-standard English. In N. Keddie (ed.), *Tinker, tailor…the myth of cultural deprivation*. Harmondsworth: Penguin.

LaPiere, R.T. (1934). Attitudes vs. actions. *Social Forces*, 13, 230-237.

Lewis, O. (1951). *Life in a Mexican village: Tepoztlan restudied*. Urbana IL: University of Illinois Press.

Liebow, E. (1967). *Tally's corner*. Boston, MA: Little, Brown.

Loftus, E.F. (2003). Our changeable memories: Legal and practical applications, *Nature*, 4, 231-234.

Maguire, M. (2000). Researching 'street criminals': A neglected art. In R.D.King & E.Wincup (eds.), *Doing research on crime and justice*. Oxford: Oxford University Press.

Mair, G. (2000). Research on community penalties. In R.D.King & E.Wincup (eds.), *Doing research on crime and justice*. Oxford: Oxford University Press.

Malinowski, B. (1922). *Argonauts of the Western Pacific*. London: George Routledge & Sons.

McGreal, C. (2011). America's crime rate is plunging, but is it really down to locking up more people? *The Guardian*, 22.08.2011.

Milgram, S. (1974). *Obedience to authority*. London: Tavistock.

Ministry of Justice. (2011). *Statistics on race and the criminal justice system*. London: National Statistics.

Parker, H., Aldridge, J. & Measham, F. (1998). *Illegal leisure: The normalisation of adolescent recreational drug use*. London: Routledge.

Parker, M. (2000). *Organisational culture and identity*. London: Sage.

Pearson, G. (1983). *Hooligan: A history of respectable fears*. Basingstoke: Macmillan.

Redfield, R. (1930). *Tepoztlan: A Mexican village*. Chicago: University of Chicago Press.

Rosenthal, R. & Jacobson, L. (1968). *Pygmalion in the classroom*. New York: Holt, Rinehart & Winston.

Russell, D. (1986). *The secret trauma: Incest in the lives of girls and women*. New York: Basic Books.

*Social Trends*. (2011). Basingstoke: Palgrave Macmillan.

Stands In Timber, J. & Liberty, M. (1967). *Cheyenne Memories*. New Haven: Yale University Press.

Venkatesh, S. (2009). *Gang leader for a day*. London: Penguin.

Walklate, S. (2000). Researching victims. In R.D.King & Wincup.E. (eds.), *Doing research on crime and justice*. Oxford: Oxford University Press.

Whyte, William F. (1955). *Street corner society* (revised edition). Chicago: University of Chicago Press.

Zimring, F.E. (2007). *The great American crime decline*. New York: Oxford University Press, Inc.